THE GREATER LEISURES

Also by Jane Miller

MANY JUNIPERS, HEARTBEATS

Jane Miller

THE GREATER LEISURES

Doubleday & Company, Inc.
Garden City, New York
1983

ACKNOWLEDGMENTS

The Agni Review: "The I Will If You Will."

The American Poetry Review: "Anonymous Meditation," "Hanging Meditation," and "Steamy Meditation."

Black Warrior Review: "Solstice."

Crazy Horse: "Like Rain in August Which Doesn't Exist," "Note to James Wright," and "The Moon Again." Originally published in *Crazy Horse.*

The Georgia Review: "The Stagger of the Wind That I Think Is Your Turning." Originally published in *The Georgia Review,* Volume XXXV, Number 1, Spring 1982.

The Iowa Review: "Three Secrets for Alexis." First appeared in *The Iowa Review,* Volume 11, Numbers 2–3, Copyright © 1981 by The University of Iowa and used by permission.

Ironwood: "East Fate."

The Nation: "Metaphysics at Lake Oswego." *The Nation* Magazine, Nation Associates, Inc.

The Seattle Review: "Troika for Lovers." First published in *The Seattle Review,* Volume IV, Number 2, Fall 1981.

Library of Congress Cataloging in Publication Data

Miller, Jane, 1949–
The greater leisures.

(The National poetry series)
I. Title.   II. Series.
PS3563.I4116G7   1983   811'.54
ISBN 0-385-18414-X
ISBN 0-385-18415-8 (pbk.)
Library of Congress Catalog Card Number 82–45601

Sonora Review: "The Song with a Hole in It," "Because You Are Flesh," and "Vivaldi's Girls."

Tendril: "Black Tea." First appeared in *Tendril Magazine.*

The Virginia Quarterly: "Green of Mildew and of Verdigris," "Mind Form," and "Graphic Meditation." Copyright © by *The Virginia Quarterly.*

Water Table: "Immense Virgin Girls," Copyright © *Water Table.*

The Arvon Foundation Poetry Competition 1980 Anthology: "Black Tea." "Contre-jour in the French Style" is named after a painting by David Hockney. I thank The Vermont Council on the Arts and The Fondation Michel Karolyi, Vence, France.

The National Poetry Series

1983

THE GREATER LEISURES, by Jane Miller (Selected by Stanley Plumly)

THE HANDS IN EXILE, by Susan Tichy (Selected by Sandra McPherson)

GOING ON Selected Poems 1958–1980, by Joanne Kyger (Selected by Robert Creeley)

CORPSE AND MIRROR, by John Yau (Selected by John Ashbery)

FROM THE ABANDONED CITIES, by Donald Revell (Selected by C. K. Williams)

to Olga Costia

CONTENTS

3

THE GREATER LEISURES

GREEN OF MILDEW AND OF VERDIGRIS

Phosphor of night-cloud, old salt freighter
sailing between sleep and wake

what was it
you said we couldn't be
eternal about

Summer leaves
hitting the window
undulations with gold-dust and brick-dust

yellow of field and fence
days of October lily
nights of algae and thrush

How animal
human eyes are
putting the ceremony back
where it belongs

Love is the best of the legend
part of a dream we live

beard-of-a-bald-man night
heavy with particulars

and russet days
whose every minute is the same
small explosions like good-bye
so that you will know me

Daily we bury the body
whose heart hasn't felt
each boat depart for nothing
sails of metal and file

On a sea of hinges
we stop our grief in the middle
to work, what we are here for

very mouth, very window, very sky

ONE

TROIKA FOR LOVERS

His gait is like he's got a cricket in his shoe;
he's lost his morning-coat.
The odd one is Mandelstam himself
laundered with a queer name in his tale.
It's the spineless and heroic victim
of *The Double*, Dostoevsky's own
equivalent for Gogol's civil servant.
They claim us in their common round
like song from a victrola
against the beefy railroad prose
which shuttles generations
like Jews from one zone to the next.

We strut Commercial St. to see *La Cage aux Folles*,
male lovers triumph over a Cultural Official;
nonetheless, his daughter marries their son.
We're alone in time.
It's our human gait.
On the beach a father taught his boy
not to catch the lines flyfishing.
Sand forms and unsettles like soldiers.
Movements may not thrust

opposites together, but a man with a strange ear might
rest his sunken face perpendicular to an era.
The sunny war lyric of Theodorakis
you honor in you new art, synthesizer.

It's a simple enough act, to bow a cymbal,
if it occurs to you
as music. We empower the odd
number we couple in, three,
cacophonous and far from the possible
which was limited and contradictory.
Men complete themselves or live on
animals. The orderly and familiar
sea drives the new gravel to lyric.
Full moon over a fast ship.
Sometimes it's as close as a string of sleep in the eye
no one else can remove, and as silent—
tradition, nothing in itself
but the dream that produced it.

THE MOON AGAIN

In Europe I love
the beach towns and trains best.
Families of ten crowd in.
Not one good set but they eat
all right. Babies slugged, husbands letting
their wives have it. Basics
aside, I like the middle class.
They stammer like birds high and fruity
first thing. Strange beds hurt
but my honey holds firm
while I light on a limb.
I won't say I don't want to change
but for some days I could die
this way. There are the honorable,
like an article I read about
Julio Cortazar not writing fantasy
for good reason. Myself, I feel
once in a while a person
has a good or a great chance
that goes unnoticed.
It begins as a sweet tooth in the palm,
baby's breath. A flower

and it's over. Only to go on
in the order of remembering:
the country lark, the night rains.
First you are meant to hear them,
then to hear of them. Damn,
who likes the mind? For one thing,
it begins and ends. In Holland
you walk it off. It's a rare day here,
lilacs sunny from heaven. Glancing back
confirms the moon again and the train
it won't separate from.

METAPHYSICS AT LAKE OSWEGO

Dawn like never before.
Rosy bands across bare trees.
For the beginner doubt and possibility both
cradle in the pink sky,
like the beginner empty and ready,
as if an egg under each arm
and without breaking them.

Ada rows out on the lake, oar-plash and bird-call.
So much in love with the music
she just moves, that's all. Great hips!
From the shore you're familiar
with her look—you must tame her
focus to see your human face.
Cradled in a boat her body

confirms destiny, already out this March
starving the deer, demanding
you dissemble and bow down
and to whom. Ada in a boat, Ada
on the shore, in the waning days of your twenties,

Ada bathing. Your whole life is overcoming
the past which is fixed

to repeat. With a kind of innocence
rustling the underbrush
you'd crawl from the spot,
red ant toward the real trees,
were she not always undressing
there before a swim. Dawn
like never before charges up

in you, alizarin, perfect and wanton
with something to express, not figure out.
You are here blindly
observing gestures again. Only when they ricochet
do the lights riddle your body:
dignity, hope.
You neither let go nor withhold.

THREE SECRETS FOR ALEXIS

Eliot's lesson from Dante
that the poet be servant

not master of language
that he attend craft

and stretch
his emotional range

omits how to
begin the awesome

first draft.
Here technique

and emotional veracity
count but

like young wheat
we care less

for an act of mind
than a good

wind and countryside.
Birds pipe supper

and through the note
pleasure somehow

translates.
Good and good in itself,

I have two lovers,
one slower than summer,

another like a sea comb,
empty and full.

I hear the old
habits of speech, for ex.,

in this country we say no
for yes

we bite into a taco
at the same time

slugging a beer.
Alexis,

eyes dreams lips and the night goes
was Pound's only line

I heard for years
because in heat its meter

undressed me. In empty space
magnetic fields exist

for no reason. How to use ideas
while living

a line, happy tension!
Quail, a missing cat,

a downpour
and two hailstorms

in one day are equal
access to knowledge

and join writers
in their separate mornings

in the beauty of an act
you spoke about,

placing a candle in a tree.
Light

in a gravitational field
falling turns bluer,

the spruce's new needles
greener

for a poem in the form of an ax.
June, July, August

three secrets
whose time we use

as in sleep
differently to imagine

our sprint and the thrush's
fear when the tree falls,

your idea
about the candle catching fire.

TIME; OR, HOW THE LINE ABOUT CHAGALL'S *LOVERS* DISAPPEARS

Man Ray is blowing out fuses in a French room
wired for minimum current.
Ours is more like a shy moment
in blue,

the pale light that witnesses three sleighs
asleep against a large pine.
So much is some distance
away:

the pond recently black with wild duck locks its inch
of ice;
and then the goose
in which a quarter of an hour is brought to despair.

Next week we shall say "three years"
as if there were such
white peaches,
in Russia, perhaps, but not here.

Here is our bedroom where doubt maintains
a yellow bedframe and, fortunately,

that spare key.
Therefore the door; we go through like Vico's spiral, like a village
moved to

tears by a passing train.
Past the effect of moonlight, if not the moon,
its steel bells interrupting the dialectic.
Your brown eyes darling, why must they be so black?

You're asleep in the fourth dimension
like an almond
tree in the mild
winter sun of the Mediterranean.

I crawl under you, careless
where destinies have a way of not sounding
serious. Speech is death
who can but laugh and pipe a flute,

who loves you.

RED FARMHOUSE WITH WHITE SKY

east through the tiny Gascon
villages the green hills of Armagnac

laughter narcissus iris rose the caves
of Lascaux bled through like rice paper

who knows but that
this moment will roll out from us

like a path that leads to a cliff
where there once were two moons temperance

and repose as you said your last
lover didn't understand

your shy moment
a drawbridge we cross

like the horizon love
it takes that long

exposure
believe me the fog

in this country you caught up on
surface

I intent on detail to make each work
better if we are willing

that long period of being
wrapped in towels at the beach

now may appear to us
foolish

arguing what
love we thought settled

onto the landscape
yellows now

south from Bordeaux into the sun
it is a common thing

the sky appears as a slow transition
when really it's the same

as us reflection
that great feeling finishing

a gesture lost on the very
young your red hair your white skin

BLACK TEA

That wedding song keeps thrumming in my head like Da Vinci's
star of Bethlehem and other sketches for plants
must have, a hundred notes on where the forest meets the field,
how the stone thirsts as if it were another being,

and your eyes that change mine in the twilight and the dawn
we confused it for. It's a secret love, and I love
standing in this field, a happy person in a field like a sweet legume
on a tongue, a kiss spiced in rain.

You could be the future because I don't know any better. Ten years
ago I was 21 and thought my body was something labial
or palatal and someone would say *silver-foil* and make me over.
You're young and can sleep

with ginger and gardenia flowers around your neck and I have to
believe you because parting is the younger sister of death
Mandelstam said. On that reprieve to Armenia under the unobserving
stars for the last time no one knew his name

was under a stone already white with a mushroom's velvety grave. *Go*
for it

the gold in his tooth said, *go* demand the dogwoods
for ten days. Damn the spring that turns to winter again, o permanent
green grass, that turquoise of your famous eyes I eat

like a cow a horse an ass awake all night, following an idea that pours
over me ice and Russian in origin. Your husky
voice ratchets an opening into a monastery, a hive with octagon
musculature. Could I take it in my hands, could I

memorize the whir of desire in this field where the tides have traveled
as if by wildflower, if by chance I could keep what for you
was a given, what for you was a simple thing, how would I settle again
onto the earth, who holds me like a child so far out

on a limb that wasn't made even for a bird. Love more fragile
than subtlety breaks habit; the natural breeze
is your hair across my back and I might have something to do with it.
The night is clear and imperfect.

Some say the stars milk themselves through the boughs of the bare
trees, and some say the trees are never bare. Some even
that these whom we counted on to remain around us like mothers,
that they aren't there. It's a good night

because you were free with me, because you let me cry on your gold
                                                                    chains
that led to my village. The two of us up there
for a look, you know the place where the sheep are born
and the goat milk is fresh, with you it felt like fruit

going back and forth across me on a silk boat, your eyelashes
suddenly bare and a message, the song
that tensed my neck with its I'm-not-a-child-anymore teeth, steamed
into worlds of wild honey. The gods are in the leaves.

MIND FORM

streaking darkness with effort
                                    —*Odysseus Elytis*

If you let July slip away
it chafes like a lover.
Glowworm and lightning storm,

the end is the same the form
surprises.
I camp here.

Saw-tooth mountains, clove,
they don't have to come to conclusion
held together by how and when.

Neither one nor the other exists
apart; not to strive after
nor word the first drop *rain*

but mind what occurs.
Who does not choose is picked.
Or, we could lie down as if

in bed. Timing and Accident.
Everyone I love makes me laugh!
Sprig of faith,

prose of evening,
Praise the Straight Road,
in an open-necked shirt,

Come Home.
I'm willing to lose you
to distraction,

that dog skunked in a shed.
I wear your clothes and wait
while the road-crew readies the night.

Like ideas
distance and pain list toward their opposite,
demand a home,

demand a mind form
power. And sway
knee-deep in a clearing of stars.

ORCHID AS IT IS LAST SEEN BEFORE
PHOTOGRAPHED AS A LAMENT

for Jorie Graham

Funny night sightseeing by bike
butter yellow loops of raw silk
drawn from cauldrons and wound slowly on a frame

                 ready for the loom

butter eggs milk pears the nostalgias
so and so in a red bandanna
so and so in bed

           we grow old and

the smallest stone held to
the light its shadow also
is a time

         breaking such as it is into English

as in 'brace yourself'
beyond the hill hills
random oaks

        who

we last called
the center of the world
drifts human high

          objects drawn from memory

if you think they are the same flowers if you love them
you are no better
than if you do not
                        one I colored blue earlier in my head

it could be any day
we get to see those eyes again
the great work waiting
                        even if it's practice

how good you look
we come to know the moment
like green meadow shock
                        after two months without sun and

26 inches of snow
the stars beautiful live ash
we don't believe dying
                        the light from the next room

casts a flower
I remember
now that it is here it seems
                        a trifle I am

waiting
no I don't think my world is created
I do something familiar
                        suddenly there's a June

HEART OF PALM

        Joyous lakes of mother and child,
pale underneaths,
           night of the hairless nights,
               random knowledge that guides
you upstairs,
        need me to live, tell me again.

Dead, is there speed enough, gradations of white enough?

        I have as we slept
              broken some of those stars off.
If I think I lose you,
         how do I make my declaration of love
       not sound perverse?

              For what I am called to, time enough?

I know because you are beautiful you are judged.
      Each particular from which I am made over, your eyes
        green as before with others, your curve
   solid as before beneath destiny.
         All beloved except the cry

that doesn't mean to look tortured nor signify
      an end.
          Fresh, harmless,

     not shy with color, spare with it,
            otherwise how know what I have touched
from what avoided.
         Lights on a bathless heaven
        starved to flower,
              let me merely turn aside and look
     good beginning.

          Stony, sandy, tree-lined,
            this our way, this our betrayal,
                  returning
    the night to its lines, limbs to their leaves,
        what's it called, a lamb, something to take in
two hands,
     the place made ready by grazing
            should the stars crave of the bird
     enough to try to land.

TWO

IMMENSE VIRGIN GIRLS

Open the door where they knock sighing.

It's a humid receptive morning.
All in voile dresses they enter:
a receiving line of obsessions,
12 sorrel horses.

They puff their gestures of regret,
sorry they aren't marmalade,
though they are, nor sponges,
wet with consolation.

Why do they breathe together like a bouquet?

Why do they amuse themselves
with mother-of-pearl necklaces?

Where did they sleep
that they awoke so many memories?

Why, with violence,
do they throw off their pretty wreaths?

12 offers and not one would renounce you.

Look at their tender repetitions,
the blue eyes of their reputations.
Immense virgin girls!

ABSTRACT ART COMPOSITION

Summer is over.
Self-consciousness begins
when the breath we take in
startles us like an intimate
moment when a door blows shut. In front of me
postcards by Matisse and Chagall.
Their girls get up from their divans to be
our fates clearly written in the sky,
two people stopping to look at stars
and then each other on those stars
and finally each other. . . .
   We go back to our places

   no longer lovers.
Identity is a mess
our unself-consciousness
sweeps up, leaving a few broomy colors
on the grid. Aside from the postcards
I receive each year from Mt. Amor, I quarrel
with love, the latent surfaces
on which it teases me until even the sky is blue

in the face. Of art you might say
there is freedom to mark a spot and learn
to forfeit it. The divan is empty
so I sit down, my next move a violet of its own.

THE GREATER LEISURES

Seasoned with heart of black sheep and in our bodies the respite
the exiled black grape, fresh water for our face and our sex,

the threshold of a great coast to which who bear
poultices bear riches, who bear sweet-smelling leaves

the maggots of a tree,
and for those who dress in this field

the evening robes our precedent
with our own smoke,

where things can suddenly be held for known
belonging to another and now inhabited upon tides I know not

yet as if coupled before the eyes of children know

*

Many omens in the way, many seeds in the way, until the hour of
                                                                evening

when pledge pure

47

like an athlete tightens the grip of a hand on a lover's
hollow of knee armpit ankle regal from harboring

Pupil of homage who takes possession
and dares not bear the fragrance of ascent

you are and so prompt
each season for love a certain hostility

Usurp the benevolent into need
I had better say if the night is in your body

and takes into its course and teaches in our name
and without the gray poppy the black queen

disgorging her god far away the palms of a strong
beating a tender glance on the waters

Better if tonight the stars are double and make of conciliation
a winter arbor of the self

for the sea too did you know comes to us branched algae
weed adrift on our lightning

the scandal of the fires of elsewhere

*

In the celebrated vat against time
the violated sweat and the flash of widows

in the blades of the shutters in the pores of the clay
in the if only and in the sincerely the chine

we shall walk out onto as mistakenly as onto a footbridge
of chimes who draws near crying

wind do not for me have had enough not for this rendezvous
to marry one winter night a little weeping with a golden rum

nor to adventure find the underside of the world's vineyard
shred and spewed out by sheep

who were a straight line to the slope of the future as rootedly
as I since you insist on

numbers and tells us to ease our ways not here not mine
liar of roads of villages of the scent itself which I was so sure of

as if I had planted the grass there and burned it

*

The unconfined the unreckoned which although familied
shadow them

like wheat forced onto desert
for the traveler is such a darkness possible breaded wormed

who has knowledge salts the someone you will die for these are the
galaxies

49

CONTRE-JOUR IN THE FRENCH STYLE

Not another hour but this hour,
not another night but here,
      plainly heard
like a bat in the house
the heart tonight, figure in the rain
in the soaked leaves of the lungs

in the ground-up glass, memory's firebox,
grand, illusory,
the assonant heart,
four-winded scape, haystacked
knoll
      flinches
by star, by strobe,
going all this way
scan and prophecy, followed, led,
practiced,
light-wound, bloodrag,

tonal, profane, heart who
habits itself to the least

movement in an act, traditional
male nude in a lit room being
strapped at the breast,
         catholic, votive, each
heart its own correspondent in the dark

pick, hammer, drum—the room full of
         perfect measure—

the homosexuals hesitate at the fine hairs of the model
         until dawn.

LIKE RAIN IN AUGUST WHICH DOESN'T EXIST

The casual violence we perform
and call 'ambiance' & the self-hate
which materializes as disdain
betray us

into a silence. I begin
writing late and drinking more—
when we dream we fly,
it's a slight jump on the rest.

The night illumines the night
with lovers half here, half-gone
over and gone over until they create
alternately lust and inhibition: the bleating

of sheep we call weakness
or else the ruth of the heavy rain.
You phrase the music
of slipping passionately down

and hate how it's only a wind
rifling carelessly through you.
I wanted to take you in
detail, hilly body, olive skin, loam,

but dammit the chafing of what is,
creek and dog language
intrude. Darkness and stars
fall intermittently. . . .

What difference
the moth who enters the flame
from the moth afraid and taken
by the silhouette?

EAST FATE

'God no' and knelt.
Sweated my hands shut

in front of my heart:
o shit, foul

glue of resin, dew, sap, steam, o
consciousness, cubes of the brain, congeal.

Who was I to have to leave
you safe, locked

into the death-feast of a silkworm
gnashing its way through the mulberry leaves?

Lucky gull, out of the sea-swell
like art out of nothing,

funny Southern vowels elegy to
part of me knows you

aren't coming back.
Not into this dilation, blue- and green-gray gone to pupil,

swivel. I saw your beautiful young face out of hearing
go.

The day will be fine.
The daisies the iris called upon so often so kind

to. be here again. In form,
the first birds return to our farm,

first manure laid down.
Heart of mine,

whose mind isn't like a harbor with oil burning
the corolla of pleasure and fear,

the islands,   .
the earliest risen?

Sleep, rest.
Sleep, wounds, scorched cities,

judgment, slave,
sleep, nothing-you-think-has-changed,

sleep's sister.
Tenderness in distance

is the death in distance
shared.

We cruised the flea market.
I kept a picture of it, Dutch clogs and chrysanthemums

behind your head. Flames,
must have been crazies welding any two finds together

for a buck. What is it in the mind
we hold to,

a rim of a hoop
we continue to fill

to trust, what can I say,
it lets us be

lovers, the door flush with being the sky,
bears time, this farm,

the return of a rose
and a black horse

boarded all winter, and in imagination
grants that we live

near the sea that one day
we may.

Come home.
Come question and exclamation,

come song.
Birds perch on our shutters

as on the rosy corners of your mouth,
without will,

they need you only
to desire.

Even among the many
we know how few we are,

waiting the season
wakes the senses, for the mind

heals that we love again
the most saturated, the milkiest,

this ward our cloud,
world. In your head

boastful and lonely
too eagerly too close

together, sun and moon. By whose light
I see you

giving in and winning. This is only how
I see it, I know,

cows, grass, summer, the chamomile
fields, the separate flares

sharply as if already here.
Can you make them out

of love? Our best
last generation couldn't and jumped

heavily down out of round.
Crazy to hike now

as it rains on the grave of a distant self,
midnight, but this is how I do it,

everything soaked into a second
consummated or forgot.

Even among the few we know
how many we are.

BECAUSE YOU ARE FLESH

Birds wake the calves
who low a little, low a little.

Wind leafs through glass to my bed.
Waiting wakes me.

There's one light on the hillside,
yours, one story I'm interested in.

It's partly a telling, partly a becoming,
like mother having to be held and told,

so long since she's been a child.
A few good years spent

looking out
for accidents yield

details: a car is a fire coming closer.
Bulldogs and cattails swell the air.

Just when there's something,
like children we beg for it

to disappear. One morning
they're painting the rowboats blue

at Owl's Head. We glide the lake
too lovely to touch down,

like after an illness you have
sensitive hearing. Some days stand out

real or not.
Two bluebirds speck the heavens and move on.

SOLSTICE

A thousand miles across Montana along the Milk River
Teddy Roosevelt said he was never out of sight
of a dead buffalo.

Buffalo Bill held Indians off by piling meat
in front of his wagon wheels,

one driver, two butchers, four mules
crouched until soldiers arrived.
He'd rush his horse into the fattest cows.

I don't want to have to think
I deliberately let them
turn back,

barely outnumbering me, my parents

hiking like vowels with shortness of breath
up the deeply-guarded secret.

Darkness purls
the long and short grass prairies,
the sentimental

disclosure of the moon, music
disfigured by dogs,
dogs by ghost and regret.

They torture the cocks off cows.

D. H. Lawrence hummed in the desert thinking about Tuscany
flowers, wild tulips on the Italian terraces,
loving each individual

petal as if it were his face struck so
by sunlight, or madness

scattered.
Otter and alcid off the cypress coast
are cut with the sickles of sails.

I ask myself over and over how to live a little
like poppies in the wind
outside a given space, how one looks

tuning an instrument, the exclamation
point finding its black beach.

NOTE TO JAMES WRIGHT

Who am I
to write this?
Shit, James Wright,
fruit, leaves, a bird,
earth now.
How does it feel lonely
where you are,
does it feel
good or what?
Last night I drank
bourbon and this morning
ate strawberries and lived
all day to 5:30
and no further.
Who am I
to stop
for you if I could
if you cared
or had time.
A photographer
today shot me
nude. May, noon,

the whole song, James
Wright, blossoms,
bees, queer high
greens and branches.
I had a chance today
to be happy
and blew it.
Sat with a book
after he left,
not dressed.
They bit me bad
the black flies,
singing. Good for you
gone, not to have
to bleed even
a little. I mean
so long. Let's say
to live
free is one note,
you're why.

THE STAGGER OF THE WIND THAT I THINK
IS YOUR TURNING

It's startling when a dog enters
the cold summer water,
and bullfrogs too, who are part
of the language, are part of the world
we drift through to remember.
We are and trail like adults
who visit their family graves, deaf
to each other while inwardly
mouthing: *one squirrel, two day-lilies, three saints.*

The spiral is natural. In Dubuffet's garden of surface,
black and white lines run like stories
that never wear shoes,
knowingly choosing
the wooded way home.
It's only a story we trust
to ourselves, how love starts us
thinking in color again, while perfectly still,
moves up the strings of the sun-rays

grazing the rose-weeds and limbs. It is,
it is like that: one day in the park you feel

proof like the hard flesh of apples
come falling. A last match is struck
and when hands take it further in,
we see ourselves in relation, smoke
the sun reddens, eyes
down, feeling the wind break
our grip.

THE SONG WITH A HOLE IN IT

They're dredging the Zuider Zee
so we remember the story,
the gentle boy plugging the wall.
He charms us on one knee
making his arrogant gesture in innocence.
Flooding is restricted now
to low areas and the last who resist
losing their island to enclosure.
The week you left we drove the coast.
Two flutes trailing a thin line.
How many can say they met
the first of Spring and saw the end
as practice, submission?
Like tulips sacrificed for
stalls set up and dismantled by dusk,
something about motion, you said,
for its own sake. The train whistling to the ferry.
To whom should I sing
of lovers waiting up to glimpse the sea,
now that you're traveling in that wine-dark
skirt toward a border? Partial eclipses,
power, pride, willfulness, fear. The train

you leave every hour on
the edge of Spring. I go back
to our cabin days, the eager run of the maple,
and out of *meanwhile* cast
the flowers and birds of our province,
our cold pine snapping
into tune. We come to remember
and to catch ourselves from falling,
that shy reminder of holes
not intending to wake during the long afternoon.
Not to mention the night,
those black bulbs you plant in my heart.

THE I WILL IF YOU WILL

Darling I'll do the deed.
We're out of water
and they say the pump's no good.
A letter from Del says
she got my note by messenger
the last day of the decade.
She wrote from Fish Creek,
can't wait to meet you and see us
catch trout and sandstone
in our shoes. You know what I mean.
She's fallen in love in no time
and thinks the Virgin River
hisses through stone beds
and love's grand and Wyoming's
a snake. I'll have to knock an inch
off the pipe and bring it closer
to earth. Then chip the ice
and hope the pump grabs
deep enough to unfreeze.
Earth's exposed where it rounds
the shed. The closer I get
to sound it, the line disappears.
I have to be alone

to love well. There's too much
or it's not there. I'm crazy
about you. Just hearing Del
dog the hills and trails
is my dowser. Home,
I'm under the house
snapping metal. You get back,
I'll give you a reason.

THREE

INFRA-RED MEDITATION

Body and memory, poles linked in rapid succession
like a woods by gunfire, by a fire sweeping just shy
of the search. Fire whose aura is a mirror of travel,

our moment of doubt, red leash on which we pull and catch
glimpses. Here the invisible, here the red squirrel was.
Glory of the fire so black at dawn, so tempting by noon,

stroked by evening. When we walk back, there are cold thighs
and the sun setting flames on the far eastern hills. Dog-fights
spot the warm snow, bitten ears. And you only felt pleasure

without passion, only remembered the lily flung down the spine
of the terrain as accident! Hateful to talk about exploits
like a dog: the only beautiful things are prompted by voices;

one acquiesces or fights. Called down the dark slope, you
have to make a lifeline out of a few flashes, glow and after-
glow, body and memory, what survives your spirited sleep.

HANGING MEDITATION

Fir limbs flaunt their icicles and the music of their fall;
the late sun tends its bruise; and we have our few questions
hazarded one evening, though they are left there like a fate

finally taken shape. O lines of the face and the tears
that wait to run down them, cats in the cedars numbed by freedom,
that dog. The moon drops its ladder and the stars flake. We hang

onto their unusual beauty, wrongly. It is only God's way
and distracting. Inside, except for the great beard, the wind,
nothing touches us. And here, like tablets in the blood, sleep

our answers. They take forever to divide night from day.
We wait our longest winter for stone to change to rain,
for risk to change our faces, rouse us, cut us down.

GRAPHIC MEDITATION

Closed lids, the violet of midnight your tilted neck.
Seen from above, this looks like sleep. A white starling
on your chest where the moon comes in. Bats, feet who

twitch. And then the hum, softly at first, almost *mama*,
the horse who enters sniffing the quilt, your hair, kingdom
of those who keep themselves from undressing. The river

unfurls from its creek and timidly the waterfowl peck
and swear. From here this sounds like a dream. On the ceiling
the prints of the horse, the already-late geese, and the owl;

tomorrow we will eat and swim and go wearing black and white
in the sun. Now let me love you to a wild call with each kiss
rejoicing its fatal leap. Lean toward me, my inscription, let me

take from you the ink of that fragrance which drives animals
to your room, that nude limit I pass each night on my way down.
Even your imprint, your shadow, gleams on my body like a psalm.

ANONYMOUS MEDITATION

for G.R.

Because I said I did and because I never did
I am now someone who has only to imagine
the evenings where the boats dock and men drink,

to live the lie again. I never meant fear
could assign me a task friendship or faith
would undo. I sang my landscape with a lament

mindful we were fifteen when we met, and now you're
crippled somewhere near New York. Courage stinks
something fierce. I'd go out to them now if I could,

if I thought leaving my rented cot
in a backward country where women are cunts
would get you up.

STEAMY MEDITATION

Canvas houses vent the cat-like peacock's *shrill.* All
settle now into the vaporous night heating its vial
of iridescent rain. Salt cache, salt belt of heat, virgin

island. Lizards, one learns, are good for killing
insects. Mosquitoes fester where we piss off the porch.
Pure eddying waters of memory, Proust, the yellow finch

who sips at our ears during naps. Underwater, the feeling
enlarged is the feeling. The last days of childhood I biked
in our basement where blue skies ripened at night. Sex is

the scorpion who disappears between floorboards to live
again as a god. Pressure in the inner ear, my self, to
steady the bike would be to steady a wave. Seas crossed

by winds turn the curving patterns we perceive, probabilities
greened. Rain and angels partly explain the parting sky.
And the waterfall turning to mist as it leans.

REVELATION AT SWIMMING HOLE

Kind Virgil quits at Canto 27, his reason
useless in Paradise.
Dante fits his sandal squarely against his ankle,
his gaze against wind.
True, he had only angels to look to,
and something akin to our century
behind. Summers we lived in the country,

asters and honeysuckle so strong
if you'd never been you could find the way cold.
Adults mind going alone.
The wind sings its vowels
and laughs like Beatrice at men
scrambling for the last word.
Or desire is a guide

and rolls the apples to the lip of the lake.
Bungalows spun when my grandfather threw me
toward God. He died a pain so great
it never hurt. Hawthorn berries,
a clot in his shirt pocket

like family converged for a swim.
From this distance dots on a scan.

Prognosis: a small heron will land
and be taken for good. *Good:*
like diving, its legacy diffuses
in concentric rings. The night
he leaves to sleep alone
never rests in its existential
bed, lights on and someone strung out

like stars. Wherever he touched me
I felt grandfather made of my body
a constellation. No one ordinary
chooses the long journey.
We like our gods camouflaged
in the morning in ferns, and ourselves
seized like a green-headed frog as it springs.

VIVALDI'S GIRLS

I give you my hand, a farmhouse with stretch to the west,
scant relief.

If there is a refrain, if we ask and are answered,
take care when you sit on the prairie.

As if you were the audience
to music not permitted
played by sixteen-year-olds, a curtain between you and them.

It's a volatile situation to walk into.

And I won't try to save you by shouting,
and I won't try to talk you to death,
a word like anyone else,

a meditation, patch of sunlight worn by the end
of summer, fabulous.
And it went down my blouse like a cube.

Ahkmatova's room after the siege,
above the unlit stove
a Modigliani

of her, one of many, the rest perished.
Taking advantage of a few minutes,

you make your first mistake:
don't lie down on the playing field.
It's October, you might knock the wind out of the wheat
        the souls are bowing.

The past alone with its metronome,
oak table, three or four chairs,
childhood on the shores of the Black Sea, Dostoevsky.

Years in which they were not seen,
snow geese flying south honk like dogs.
The life of the unlanguaged

birds in flight, as in thought,
what they meant as they said no:

we can stop anytime we want
if we think we hear a song.

Young-o.

UNACCOMPANIED

Beautifully sifted
soft light through the lunette,
                    a slice of orange, redwood bark,
and covered me as silt, as rouge,
as bandage.
                    Like I see the snow I see now
full of meaning
the resins the roses
                    and the twilights we made of our eyes
closing,
trying to live forever for a few hours.
                    I do no harm thinking of you.
Cyclamen in the green windowbox,
I want to think you remember them too—
                    so complicated!
to give up the original for what
is beautiful,
                    that time we cancelled and call Saturday.
Everything deserves a name.
Leaves, stems, peels, blossoms
                    I crush nearer my nose,

I cross your pond again
with the great ease of serious effort:
                   with my eyes.
All this work, is it that we have to
appreciate to create
                   that sedge insect and wall
in the shade of the beautiful
house sought for its southern light,
                   worthless and charming,
like lovers in snow
crossing unposted land without thinking
                   what they are subject to.

MILK LAKE

You wouldn't know it
for the fog, you wouldn't, except
                        a small fire
            hardly noticed let
                        alone, I have your drawing here
                                    otherwise
the room is white. Because we are full of feeling,
            white and clear between rain—
                                    a deer shot caught in fence, gruesome,
                                    in the head—
                                                not the brambles we curse
                                                            nor cleave—
need as part of a crisis,
            as a bee makes honey the silence
                        this is hard,
to plunge into winter with a future:
                        approach, enthusiasm,
                                                two girls!

Omphalos rock embarrassed at low tide,
            Chinese lanterns the swinging flame and its opposite
                        sun.

I am about nineteen today in my
                    head
digging agate, spewing like
                    a wet dog
the practice all for nothing
          my own circumstance and not the historical.
     You walk below me
                         a small red sky.
Hope is young,
          map-making with hairs so strong
and soft the figures
          "I think of you often."

TULIPS FOR TWO AND FOUR HANDS

boats an alphabet in the canal
something painted in our name

a few prostitutes
who I thought

mannequins at first
bent their knees

horses working
the streets steamed

like a night bath
or a poem about smoke

moon and icicles
or a photograph

some with your fear
giving way to color

have faded
like when you said

there's nothing like the truth
to open the evening

we have separate lives
even turned

toward you
let me

see behind you
the raised slips of the waves

*

far from home with its small
'm' one could rest on like a loveseat

the endless water that surfaces
from below land

disappearing and being reclaimed
the tiny music of ships in bottles

what Braque calls
the fortuitous

all of us versions
virgins

loosening and losing
to the thirst of the salt

like an island in my flesh
I remembered

being shoved into a lake
saying *gallop gallop*

and slapping my heart
the same that thanks

the sides of cows in this dairy region
a distant part of me

catches
on the milky stars the ritual

carving of the blonde heads of cheese
your homeland for the first time

surrounded by ideas
Hart Crane accompanying himself with ship-bells

some on the other side of this world

*

as we took the curve
north across a few bridges

a narrow slat separated
a village on stilts from the sea

bicycles slept openly
signs disclaimed about the morning

sale of truck-sized wheels of edam and gouda
out of place for a time

like evening in white-face
and 17th century dress a couple

huddled and trained to the edge
as if they were the foreigners

as if there were someone
I could trust

to say these things for me
and we were the secrets of families

a pack of dogs
out god help me as I have always wanted

to imagine the dark green lining of the moon
once we got it in sight

*

it's only paper-folding
for beginners the season shuffles

its coarse hairs and wire
Dubuffets sprawl outdoors

the pond a plastic
reflection and shade

I test my head on the head of a Buddha
you focus and kneel

our faces in the tulip fields
in our cups in the restaurant

thick with lipstick and rouge
a few Van Goghs we'd never seen

his unfinished fit of blue and azure
his hospital

the simple balconies covering with snow
the urge to build

peace out of time
so what if I'm one figure

being woven on a loom
brushing the blouse of the weaver

the desire to take you
the humor of mobiles

the utter fairness of glass
this music of the rocks

barely all my life
as the first star is scout

into the night like beads across the abacus
stretched out even willing

THE SPARROWS WE WEEP WE SEE

Driving for hours
and still morning: the princess' white undergarments!
It seems we were the only _____.
Imperceptible is the soul
coming to request,
like a lover
in you as if to find the smallest star
for which the constellation is named:

Lorca somewhere else,
sun going-down-like
on a woman rolling
my eyes back, fucked
by tongue,
the secret-myself-away, though there are names for it
and tensions turn that way.
Having fallen, not in English, no,
the petals tear, the sands, uncomfortable, tilt,
a negro landscape, I have gone, I was going, I go,
and the scents and dusts burn unnoticed.
Burn.

Black sun, yellow rocks, sand, no,
black rocks, sun, yellow sand . . .
strange, monumental,
                    a day of
look, trees, clouds, sky.
White caps stop 200 yards out
and apron a sound like the lagoon opposite,
its slavish rocks holding unsteadily,
doing their jobs poorly and giddy besides. . . .
One sail, birds soaring of a piece,
                    how many birds?
thank yous,
the partings we call joy.

Jane Miller was born in New York in 1949. She has lived in Northern California, Iowa, Vermont, and Greece. Her work has appeared in *Antaeus* and *The American Poetry Review*, among other periodicals. She is a recipient of The Discovery Award, from the YM-YWHA/*The Nation*, and has received grants from The Vermont Council on the Arts and The Fondation Michel Karolyi. She is now living on Cape Cod.